JOHN F. KENNEDY

The Presidents of the United States

George Washington
1789–1797

John Adams
1797–1801

Thomas Jefferson
1801–1809

James Madison
1809–1817

James Monroe
1817–1825

John Quincy Adams
1825–1829

Andrew Jackson
1829–1837

Martin Van Buren
1837–1841

William Henry Harrison
1841

John Tyler
1841–1845

James Polk
1845–1849

Zachary Taylor
1849–1850

Millard Fillmore
1850–1853

Franklin Pierce
1853–1857

James Buchanan
1857–1861

Abraham Lincoln
1861–1865

Andrew Johnson
1865–1869

Ulysses S. Grant
1869–1877

Rutherford B. Hayes
1877–1881

James Garfield
1881

Chester Arthur
1881–1885

Grover Cleveland
1885–1889

Benjamin Harrison
1889–1893

Grover Cleveland
1893–1897

William McKinley
1897–1901

Theodore Roosevelt
1901–1909

William H. Taft
1909–1913

Woodrow Wilson
1913–1921

Warren Harding
1921–1923

Calvin Coolidge
1923–1929

Herbert Hoover
1929–1933

Franklin D. Roosevelt
1933–1945

Harry Truman
1945–1953

Dwight Eisenhower
1953–1961

John F. Kennedy
1961–1963

Lyndon B. Johnson
1963–1969

Richard Nixon
1969–1974

Gerald Ford
1974–1977

Jimmy Carter
1977–1981

Ronald Reagan
1981–1989

George H. W. Bush
1989–1993

William J. Clinton
1993–2001

George W. Bush
2001–2009

Barack Obama
2009–

JOHN F. KENNEDY

WIL MARA

Marshall Cavendish
Benchmark
New York

Marshall Cavendish Benchmark
99 White Plains Road
Tarrytown, NY 10591
www.marshallcavendish.us

All Internet addresses were correct at the time of printing.

Library of Congress Cataloging-in-Publication Data

Mara, Wil.
John F. Kennedy / by Wil Mara.
p. cm. — (Presidents and their times)
Summary: "Provides comprehensive information on President John F. Kennedy and places
him within his historical and cultural context. Also explored are the formative events of his
times and how he responded"—Provided by publisher.
Includes bibliographical references and index.
ISBN 978-0-7614-3628-7
1. Kennedy, John F. (John Fitzgerald), 1917–1963—Juvenile literature. 2. Presidents—
United States—Biography—Juvenile literature. 3. United States—Politics and
government—1961–1963—Juvenile literature. I. Title.
E842.Z9M368 2010
973.922092—dc22
[B]
2008033242

Editor: Christine Florie
Publisher: Michelle Bisson
Art Director: Anahid Hamparian
Series Designer: Alex Ferrari

Photo research by Connie Gardner

Cover photo by The Granger Collection

The photographs in this book are used by permission and through the courtesy of:
Getty Images: Time and Life Pictures, 3, 8, 40, 46, 55, 60, 61, 64, 70, 71, 90, 97, 99 (R);
Popperfoto, 10, 84; Fox Photos/Stringer, 18; Getty Images, 21, 66; Hulton Archive, 36,
44, 60, 99 (L); Sanford Kossin, 81; *The Granger Collection:* 47; *Image Works:* Schert/
Sueddeutsche Zeitung Photo, 13; *Corbis:* Bettmann, 14, 23, 33, 49, 51, 53, 74, 77,
92, 95, 98 (R), 99 (L), Tom Dillard/Dallas Morning News, 93; *AP Photo:* 31.

Printed in Malaysia
1 3 5 6 4 2

CONTENTS

John F. Kennedy was the youngest person to be elected president of the United States. His presidency was viewed by many as a time of new hope.

The gleaming, midnight-blue limousine rolled slowly down another corridor of tall buildings. The top had been removed, making it look like a family convertible on a Sunday drive. But then it was a clear and sunny day, perfect for late November.

In the back of the limo sat John F. Kennedy, America's thirty-fifth president. Women adored him, men wanted to be like him. He was handsome, intelligent, and witty, yet humble and compassionate. They were saying he was one of the best presidents the nation had ever seen, young and fresh and full of new ideas. With his beautiful wife and two adorable children, he created a certain feeling in the White House. People had come to call it **Camelot**, after the court of the legendary King Arthur, who fought for virtues such as bravery and honor and courage. This president seemed to have all those qualities.

The streets were filled with thousands of admirers, waving and clapping and taking pictures. They called out to Kennedy, hoping he would meet their gaze and wave back. He had a naturally friendly way about him. He was in Dallas, Texas, because the next presidential election was coming up, and he had barely received enough votes to win Texas during the 1960 presidential election. He needed to let the people of Texas know he cared about them even though he'd been born far away in Massachusetts. He was the president of all Americans.

The limousine made a right turn and rode briefly past a seven-story warehouse that was used to store textbooks. Then it made another left that cut through an open plaza. More people stood along the landscape, clicking their cameras, waving little flags, and trying to get the president's attention. The governor of Texas and his wife were sitting in the seat in front of the Kennedys. When the governor's wife turned and made a comment about the crowd's friendly welcome, the president smiled and agreed. Then the unthinkable happened. . . .

EARLY DAYS

John Fitzgerald Kennedy was born on May 29, 1917, in Brookline, Massachusetts, to a solid middle-class home. He was the second son of Joseph P. "Joe" Kennedy Sr. and Rose Fitzgerald Kennedy. Joe was a very driven and ambitious man, proud of his Irish background. When he wanted something, he let nothing stand in his way. This fighting spirit came from being looked down upon by those in the New England area who felt the Irish were beneath them. Joseph Kennedy was deeply resentful of this, and he had every intention of making sure his family held a place of power and respect in society. Much of Joe's toughness came from his own father, Pat, as noted by biographer Ted Schwarz: "He was similar to Pat in both temperament and ethics. They were ruthless men who would take whatever action was necessary

Joseph and Rose Kennedy raised nine children, several of whom eventually entered the nation's political scene.

Irish Heritage

Kennedy's ancestry was Irish on both sides. His middle name, in fact, honored Rose's family, the Fitzgeralds. The two families had come from Ireland three generations earlier, in the mid-nineteenth century, to seek a better life in America. Kennedy's paternal great-grandfather, for example, repaired barrels and casks and lived in a tenement house, while his maternal great-grandfather worked on a farm. It was difficult for people of Irish heritage to earn high regard in society back then, particularly in the New England area. But the Kennedys and the Fitzgeralds worked hard, saved their money, and eventually became store owners, landholders, and politicians. Joseph and Rose upheld the Irish tradition of large families: they had five daughters and four sons.

to achieve or maintain power." Pat Kennedy's son would eventually accumulate tremendous wealth, but he wanted his children to keep reaching higher and achieve great things. His impact on the life of his son John was deep and long lasting.

Another important, although unfortunate, part of John's life was a string of health problems. As a boy, he spent more than two months in the hospital with scarlet fever. He also had a severe case of chicken pox, plus numerous infections of the inner-ear. He had appendicitis at the age of thirteen and required surgery, which left him bedridden for awhile. He suffered multiple flulike colds during his first year of high school, which were made worse because he never seemed to put on much weight.

Even though he bounced back from each of these ailments, poor health would always be a problem—and it would haunt his mind as well. Once, when a friend scolded him for being too concerned about acquiring a good tan, Kennedy replied, "Well . . . it's not only that I want to look that way, but it makes me feel that way. It gives me confidence, it makes me feel healthy. It makes me feel healthy, strong, attractive."

John F. Kennedy's youth was marred by health issues. Here he is photographed around age eight.

THE UNSTEADY STUDENT

As a youngster, Kennedy's performance in school was unsteady. One year he would do well, in another his parents would receive warning notes from concerned teachers and administrators. It wasn't that little "Jack" wasn't intelligent, they said—he just wasn't trying hard enough. "Can do better" or "Is working below his abilities" were typical comments. The fact that the Kennedy family moved several times during this period didn't help, either. From kindergarten through eighth grade, the future president went to five different schools.

Kennedy's grades didn't improve much during his freshman and sophomore years of high school. In September 1931 he began attending Choate, a private school in Connecticut. Kennedy's older brother, Joe Jr., had already been there for two years and was one of the school's best students. This put extra pressure on Jack to do well, yet he didn't possess his older brother's willingness to adhere to rules or respect authority. Choate was a place of structure and discipline, and Kennedy was always free-spirited. He would show up for classes late, forget to bring his books, and make jokes about his teachers. The school's headmaster complained to Kennedy's parents, causing them to fear that their son might be expelled.

What Kennedy lacked in conformity, however, was balanced by a rare gift that would serve him well in the years ahead—tremendous charm. He was very popular with his fellow students, making them laugh and showing kindness and loyalty. He was also becoming very handsome. He quickly learned how to use all these advantages, and Choate's headmaster eventually changed his opinion of him, "the more I talk with him, the more confidence I have in him," and "I never saw a boy with as many fine qualities as Jack has that didn't come out right . . . in the end." He even said that while Jack's independence was sometimes a burden on the school, it might enable him to achieve great things one day.

THE GREAT DEPRESSION

Even though Jack didn't have a burning passion for schoolwork, he did develop a curiosity about current events. Other students remember that he always seemed to know what was going on in the world. Kennedy read *The New York Times* every day, and he could often be found listening to news reports on the radio. A girl he once dated remembered him becoming angry because she had turned off his car radio while he was listening to it. This era in his life marked the beginning of a new chapter—his interest in public affairs.

The most significant event in America during Jack's time in high school was probably the **Great Depression**. World War I (1914–1918) had left most of Europe, as well as parts of Asia and Africa, in ruins. During the war, American farmers enjoyed a bustling business because they were able to sell their products to many overseas nations. Now that the same nations had to focus on rebuilding themselves, American farmers made less money. Many farmers had borrowed from American banks to buy equipment and more farmland to keep up with the wartime demand. Now they were unable to make payments on those loans.

Also, the average American citizen had discovered a new way of buying products and services through a system called credit. With credit, you could take possession of something now and pay for it later. Most Americans loved the credit plan, as it allowed them to live the good life without necessarily being able to afford it. America was manufacturing lots of interesting new products, from cars to furniture to household appliances, and everyone wanted to get in on the fun.

Between the banks losing money because the farmers couldn't pay off their loans and other people using credit to acquire things they couldn't otherwise have afforded, the American financial system reached a breaking point. The worst of it began on Thursday, October 24, 1929 (a date that would become known as Black Thursday), and hit a climax on Tuesday, October 29, 1929, when the value of American stocks fell about 80 percent. People lost millions—those who had been rich were now broke, and those who were already poor became poorer. The economy continued to sink for years to come, and by 1933 one-third of all adults couldn't find a job. People who once had homes, cars, and money in a savings account were living on the streets and begging for food. And since America's economy was so closely tied to the economies of other major nations, the rest of the world suffered as well.

One person who was not adversely affected by the Great Depression, however, was Joe Kennedy Sr. He had put his money in safe places and avoided the suffering. As his biographer Ted Schwarz put it, "Joe Kennedy was a greedy man, but he was not a fool. He liked investing in sure things." Jack, as a result, would never experience the Depression firsthand.

Many people lost their jobs and homes during the Great Depression. In the New York City scene shown here, many unemployed people have set up shelter in a place called "Hardluck Town."

Instead, he would learn about it through reports on radio, television, and in newspapers. For him, it was like reading a passage from a history book—a tragedy that was happening to other people in other places.

COLLEGE DAYS

Jack graduated from Choate in June 1935 and, after a brief trip to Europe that summer, applied for late admission to Princeton University. Because Jack's admission request was so late, however, it was denied. Jack then contacted his father, who quickly fixed the situation by calling Princeton and talking to some people. This kind of "pulling of strings" would become a familiar pattern with Joe Kennedy Sr. Ironically, the Princeton effort would ultimately be wasted—Jack started there in early November 1935, but became ill the following month and had to be hospitalized. Then, on the advice of his doctors, he spent the first half of 1936 in Arizona to recuperate in its warmer climate. While there, he decided to take classes at Harvard University in Cambridge, Massachusetts.

John F. Kennedy graduated from Choate, a private school in Connecticut in June 1935 .

Kennedy's first two years at Harvard were, in many ways, similar to his time at Choate—he was an average student who fell short of his potential while making many friends.

BROTHERLY COMPETITION

Princeton was one of the finest colleges in the world, but Jack may have chosen to go there instead of Harvard simply because his brother Joe was already at Harvard and doing well. Jack and Joe were highly competitive with each other. Joe, being the oldest, often taunted and antagonized Jack in their younger years. He would bully Jack mercilessly, taking advantage of Jack's weak physical condition. While this was cruel, it also motivated Jack to push himself harder. On the other hand, it also made Jack feel as though he was always standing in his brother's long shadow.

His attitude toward his studies changed, however, when he visited his father in London in July 1938. The senior Kennedy had been named ambassador to Britain's Court of St. James by President Franklin Delano Roosevelt. The appointment gave the Kennedy family a kind of "royal air," and Jack was treated like an aristocrat. He stayed in mansions, ate in the finest restaurants, and attended the private parties of English society's wealthiest people.

He also experienced some of the current events that he had previously only been hearing and reading about. For example, he and his family had to leave London for the south of France because of rising tensions between England and Germany. German leader Adolf Hitler had already invaded Austria, and he wanted Czechoslovakia next. His ultimate goal, many believed, was the conquest of Europe—and possibly the world.

A Turning Point

Kennedy returned to Harvard that fall a changed man. The European experience had fired his imagination. He immediately improved as a student, and he requested permission from the school to take time off to return to Europe and begin researching and writing a thesis on current affairs in the region. In February 1939 he received permission, whereupon he traveled between several European nations, filling notebooks and talking with hundreds of people.

The student researcher was forced to end his trip in late September when Adolf Hitler ordered his military forces to invade Poland, for it was clear that England would declare war on Germany in response. The Kennedy family was invited to sit in the parliamentary chamber as Britain's leaders spoke about the difficult decisions ahead. He listened carefully to Prime Minister Neville Chamberlain and was particularly impressed by First Lord of the Admiralty Winston Churchill, who would soon replace Chamberlain.

Kennedy returned to Harvard in the fall of 1939 and threw himself into his studies. Almost all his courses had to do with government, current events, or international affairs. He had a specific interest in international affairs, believing that increased travel and advances in communications were pulling the world closer together. As he studied different forms of government and political philosophy, the rich kid who had had a reputation for laziness began challenging his professors with questions and ideas of his own.

He also continued working on his thesis, which now focused on his concern that England was responding too slowly to the growing threat from Adolf Hitler, particularly in terms of building up the country's military to keep pace with Germany's. The paper's title, "Appeasement at Munich," referred to the agreement signed in that city in September 1938 by Germany, England, France, and Italy. The Munich Pact essentially handed Hitler parts of Czechoslovakia in return for a promise not to invade other parts of Europe.

Despite problems with organization, style, and grammar, Kennedy's thesis did impress many with its mature opinions and observations. When Hitler ignored the promise he had made in Munich and began his campaign to conquer all of Europe, people began to talk about "Appeasement at Munich." Kennedy updated the work, and his father arranged for it to be published as a book with a new title, suggested by *New York Times* journalist Arthur Krock—*Why England Slept*. It became a huge hit around the world.

Jack graduated from Harvard in June 1940 with a degree in international affairs. In spite of having wealth, good looks, a highly influential father, a degree from one of the best schools in the world, and a best-selling book, he was unsure of what to do next. Suffering from a digestive ailment and severe back problems, he decided to go to California, where, as in Arizona, the weather was warmer. He then enrolled at Stanford in September 1940 to study business.

But his Stanford days would be as short-lived as his attendance at Princeton. He left in December and returned home, first to help his father write a book of his own, then to do some traveling throughout South America. Next, he gave some thought to enrolling in law school. Then he decided on something else— there was a war going on in Europe and Asia, and since America was probably going to get involved, he wanted to be a part of it.

NAVAL MAN

After World War I, Hitler's home country of Germany had been forced to sign an agreement known as the Treaty of Versailles. The treaty required Germany not only to admit blame for the outbreak of the war, but also to pay for most of the damage (at a cost of more than $30 billion), to give up much of its power elsewhere in Europe and in Africa, and to reduce the national military to almost nothing. As a result of the war, and the treaty requirements, the German economy was nearly driven to total ruin.

Adolf Hitler became active in Germany's political scene after World War I. He was elected the country's chancellor in 1933.

As ordinary Germans suffered through the 1930s, Hitler appeared as a new figure on the political scene. He was infuriated by the Treaty of Versailles and by his country's failure to oppose it vigoursly. In his book *Mein Kampf (My Struggle)*, Hitler wrote, "In 1919, when the Peace Treaty was imposed on the German nation, there were grounds for hoping that this instrument of unrestricted oppression would help to reinforce the outcry for the freedom of Germany." While other German leaders did little to improve conditions in the country, Hitler promised sweeping changes that would bring Germany back to its former glory. The people liked what they heard, and Hitler was elected chancellor in 1933. Soon thereafter, he eliminated opposition to his policies by outlawing all political parties other than his own. Then he began rebuilding the German military. Remilitarization was in violation of the Treaty of Versailles, but neither Hitler nor the German people cared, and no other nations tried to stop him.

Around the same time, the Asian nation of Japan was looking to expand its own empire. It had been one of the winners of

A Decorated Veteran

Adolf Hitler participated in World War I as a corporal in an infantry regiment. He was assigned the dangerous job of being a runner—carrying important messages from place to place, often under the hail of enemy fire. By all reports, he was a reliable soldier, following orders without question and showing uncommon bravery. By war's end, he had won two medals and a badge for a wound in the leg. In spite of these personal accomplishments, he was devastated by his country's loss of the war. He believed the German people were destined not only to win victory in Europe, but ultimately to rule the world—a dream that would eventually take the lives of millions and give Adolf Hitler his place as one of the most nightmarish figures in human history.

World War I, and, as a result, had become very powerful. In the 1930s Japan began invading parts of nearby China with the ambition of conquering the entire country and then moving on to others. Hitler followed a similar course in 1939, using his well-trained military to overrun Denmark, Norway, Belgium, Luxembourg, and the Netherlands in a span of just three months. France was next, which Hitler toppled with help from Italy, under the dictatorship of his friend and ally Benito Mussolini. By 1941 Germany, Italy, and Japan had signed a pact to help fulfill their joint ambitions, and World War II was under way.

The president of the United States, Franklin D. Roosevelt, struggled with the decision of U.S. involvement in the war in Europe. He was happy to sell military equipment to the nations fighting against Germany, Italy, and Japan. But initially he was hesitant to send troops. This hesitation ended on December 7, 1941, when more than 360 Japanese planes carried out a surprise bombing campaign on an American naval base in Hawaii called Pearl Harbor. More than 2,300 American soldiers and citizens were killed while nine ships sank and more than twenty others were heavily damaged. The next day, the United States declared war on Japan, Germany, and Italy.

Kennedy Signs Up

The idea of Jack Kennedy serving in the military probably seemed absurd to those who knew him best. Candidates for service were required to pass several physical tests to gain admittance into the armed forces, and Kennedy had so many health problems and such a bad medical history that his chances were all but zero.

He failed the physical exams for both the army and the navy in the spring of 1941. But, as was the Kennedy way, that didn't

The USS Arizona *burns during the bombing of Pearl Harbor on December 7, 1941.*

mean he gave up. Throughout the summer, he put himself through a grueling fitness program. And, once again, his father stepped in to help. He contacted an old friend who held a high position in the navy. That man saw to it that Kennedy received a relatively clean bill of health and that he would have a position waiting for him in military intelligence in Washington, D.C.

Jack was assigned to rewrite news stories so they could be used in intelligence briefings. That meant sitting at a desk and typing all day—boring for someone as active, intelligent, and free-spirited as Kennedy, and also painful due to his bad back.

These two factors, coupled with the Japanese attack on Pearl Harbor made Kennedy itch for more important duty. After America officially entered World War II, he wanted to be part of the action.

PT COMMANDER

In the summer of 1942 Kennedy began training for assignment on a patrol torpedo (PT) boat. Small in comparison to other military vessels, PT boats were useful in attacking enemy ships. They carried heavy ammunition, and they were difficult to hit. A certain amount of hype had built up around the PTs, particularly in the American media, where heroic war stories were welcomed by the public. The PTs were "the little boats that could," and Kennedy saw the chance to both participate in battle and be part of a glamorous, elite group. He would later say, "I worked hard at it because I liked PTs. I think I liked [them] because they were small. I don't think I gave much thought to world conditions and things during the war. Some, of course, but not much." In particular, he wanted to command one of the PTs, and luckily, this was a common assignment for Ivy Leaguers with boating experience.

Ironically, his father now became a barrier rather than an aid to him—Joe Sr. was concerned for Jack's life. So, following PT training, the elder Kennedy made sure that Jack was assigned to train others. Naturally, he didn't like this assignment, and, displaying a gritty determination that reflected his father's, he found a way to get what he wanted—he asked his maternal grandfather, who was also powerful and well connected, to help him out. After some phone calls, Jack was transferred to the Solomon Islands in the southern Pacific Ocean in the spring of 1943. He was eventually given command of a boat called *PT 109*.

For the first few months of duty, Kennedy and his crew saw little action on *PT 109*. They were ordered to move from island to island, mostly to wait for Japanese ships that they could attack. During this period, Kennedy developed a very different view of the PTs from that of the hype—he decided that they were poorly built, poorly equipped, and poorly commanded at the top level. While his own men seemed loyal to him, those in other PT crews

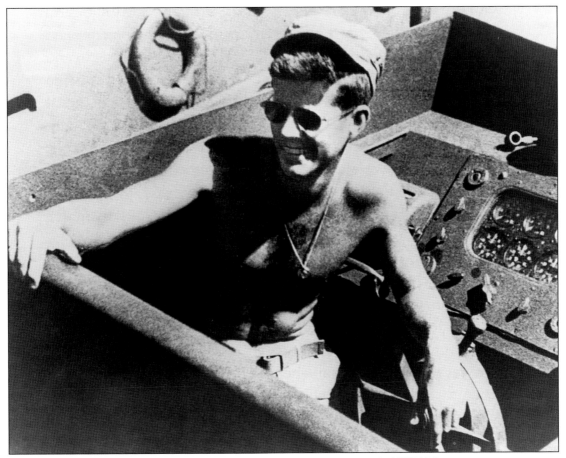

While serving in the navy during World War II, Kennedy commanded PT 109.

were lazy and undisciplined—making for a potentially dangerous situation, since there is little room for carelessness in wartime. Nevertheless, Kennedy vowed to do the best he could with his own boat and the men at his command.

On one occasion, Kennedy bravely led his crew to safety and rescue after a tragic accident. The story of his heroics made headlines across America, and the PT boat's commander became the main focus, since his name was already well-known. When interviewed, his crew talked about their officer's courage and leadership. The Kennedy family, of course, could not have been prouder, particularly when Jack was awarded the Navy and Marine Corps Medal. Even his older brother, Joe Jr., set aside their rivalry and praised him. The story made for excellent reading back in the States, particularly when the public noted that Jack had come from a privileged background yet chose to put himself in harm's way. Robert Donovan, an author who would later write a book about the *PT 109* incident, said, "I talked to everyone in his crew, and those men would do anything for Kennedy. There is no question that Kennedy was brave, that he saved that crewman's life."

Kennedy displayed a characteristic modesty in the face of all this attention, pointing out the courage and endurance of the other survivors. His humility only endeared him further to American citizens. Privately, Kennedy was angered about the whole affair and wanted revenge against the Japanese. He was particularly bitter about the two deaths that occurred under his command.

His bitterness increased when Joe Jr. was unexpectedly killed on August 12. Also a serviceman, Kennedy's older brother had volunteered for a dangerous mission—to pilot a

A Wartime First

On August 1, 1943, *PT 109* and fourteen other PTs were ordered to carry out a night attack on a group of Japanese destroyers in a channel known as the Blackett Strait, located in the Solomon Islands. The mission was supposed to be a carefully coordinated effort, with four of the PTs leading the charge because they had the radar equipment needed to locate the enemy ships on a pitch-black night. But some PTs failed to fire their weaponry, others fled in fear, and those with the crucial radar gear left the area too early, preventing the vessels without radar from navigating effectively.

In the midst of this debacle, Kennedy's boat made military history when it became the only PT in World War II to be struck by an enemy vessel—a Japanese destroyer named the *Amagiri* sliced it in half. Two of Kennedy's crew—one man who had been with him since the beginning of his command and the other only nineteen years old and recently assigned—were killed. These deaths rattled Kennedy and would haunt him for years to come. At the time, however, he managed to stay focused on the more important issue—leading the ten survivors to safety. They clung to the hull, which remained afloat because it had several water-tight compartments. They were hesitant to approach any of the nearby islands for fear of possible Japanese occupation. But they also knew they couldn't stay in the water forever.

(continued)

They reached a tiny strip of land—about the size of a football field—called Plum Pudding Island. One member of the crew had been severely burned and couldn't swim, so Kennedy dragged him along with the strap of the man's life vest between his teeth. Plum Pudding Island was a good distance away, and the journey took five grueling hours. Kennedy then swam to a nearby channel and tried, unsuccessfully, to catch the attention of any passing American vessel. By this point he was exhausted and had to rest. Another crew member tried the same thing the following night, also without success. The next day, the starving crew swam to another island—Olasana—in the hope of finding fresh water and food. All they could locate were coconuts. But they also encountered two friendly Solomon Islanders. Kennedy scratched a message into a coconut shell and asked the local men to take it to the base of the PT boats, which they did. Within two days, all of the remaining survivors had been rescued.

plane full of explosives with the objective of ramming it into an enemy outpost. Possibly he wanted take such a huge risk to compete with Jack's heroics on *PT 109*. Whatever the motivation, something went terribly wrong—he was supposed to eject from the plane shortly before impact, and a plane flying close behind would detonate the explosives with an electronic remote control. But Joe's plane exploded prematurely; he was killed instantly.

Joe's death sent shock waves throughout the Kennedy family. Joe Sr. was devastated, having spent much of his life creating opportunities and making big plans for his oldest son. Presidential biographer Arthur Krock said that Joe Jr.'s death caused ". . . one of the most severe shocks to the father that I've ever seen registered on a human being." Jack was also crushed, for despite their fierce competitiveness, there was also a genuine affection between the brothers.

This blow to his spirit, plus the fact that the *PT 109* incident had further damaged his already frail body, didn't stop Jack from returning to duty in late August. He contributed to several effective attacks against enemy ships, which probably gave him some satisfaction. In spite of this renewed passion, however, the physical strain simply became too great. By winter, he had developed stomach ulcers, and his back was causing unbearable pain. An operation for the back pain was strongly recommended by his doctors. Although Kennedy put it off as long as possible, he was admitted for surgery in June 1944. He recovered slowly, and other medical problems continued to plague him. In March 1945 he was officially retired from the U.S. Navy.

EARLY POLITICAL CAREER

$\mathcal{K}$ennedy's interest in political affairs had not diminished during his military service. If anything, his time overseas increased his sense of global issues. After he returned home, he went to great pains to educate himself on **domestic** issues as well. He and his father believed that high-ranking members of the U.S. government would hold positions of tremendous power, influence, and affluence in the years ahead.

World War II didn't last long after Kennedy's exit from the navy. In 1942 both Germany and Japan had begun losing important battles, and by 1944 the countries that had been fighting against them were regaining much of the ground they had lost. In April 1945 forces of the Soviet Union—which had been fighting alongside America and several other nations—entered the German capital of Berlin. Hitler, hiding in an underground bunker, chose to commit suicide rather than risk being captured. The following September, Japanese forces surrendered, marking the end of World War II.

Following a long rehabilitation period, Kennedy took a temporary job as a reporter for the *Chicago Herald-American*. He covered various political events for the newspaper, gaining access to important people. He went to the first United Nations conference in San Francisco and then to Europe to write about the aftermath of World War II. He came away from these experiences more determined than ever to have a career in public service. As he saw it, a reporter merely witnessed the process of governing, whereas a politician took part in it.

Rough Road to Congress

In planning his first move, Kennedy considered trying for state office. His father was on good terms with Massachusetts governor Maurice Tobin, who would be up for reelection in 1946 and would need a running mate. But a national position had more appeal—Kennedy wanted to get to Washington, D.C., where he would be on course for bigger things down the road. So he and

The Kid Congressman

One of the biggest obstacles in Kennedy's early political career was the view shared by many that he was just a kid, even after he had won his first race. In fact, he had a very youthful look about him, more like a college student than an elected official. Once, while supporting President Truman at a rally, Kennedy was mistaken for an ordinary onlooker by agents of the Secret Service, who had to be told that he was really a congressman. Another time, while visiting Harvard, he was mistaken for a student and asked to take part in a football practice. Good-natured as always, Kennedy joined the workout for a bit until a surprised coach identified him.

his father set their sights on a seat in the **House of Representatives**. Specifically, they decided to go after the seat from Massachusetts Eleventh District, which was going to be vacant for the 1946 election.

The problem, of course, was that Kennedy wasn't the only person who wanted the congressional seat. It wasn't a matter of running against the eventual **Republican Party** challenger, since the district was overwhelmingly populated with voters who reliably supported the **Democratic Party**. It was another Democrat—a prominent local politician named Mike Neville—who also wanted the seat. Neville had a lot of influence in the area, and the newspapers pounded Kennedy for being young and inexperienced, for being wealthy in an area where most voters were lower and middle class, and for not being born and raised locally and therefore even less able to relate to the people in the district and their problems.

But Kennedy forged ahead. In fact, when he was attacked, his natural competitiveness rose to the surface. Although he was not comfortable as a public speaker, he learned the value of a stirring speech and the proper way to deliver it. "He was always shy," remembered Mark Dalton, a fellow politician and Kennedy friend. "He drove himself into [politics]. It must have been a tremendous effort of will." He was also something of a loner, yet he trained himself to walk out in public and introduce himself to complete strangers. He would explain his position on important issues, then listen as people offered their own thoughts. He had a charm and an easiness that ordinary folks found appealing. He was also humble about his war record, which impressed many of the blue-collar voters, who often were veterans themselves or had relatives or friends who had served.

Kennedy joins volunteers at one of his campaign headquarters in 1946. He served as a Massachusetts congressman from 1947 to 1953.

The campaign schedule was brutal on the sickly young man. A sixteen-hour day was not unusual, with Kennedy up at sunrise and not returning to bed until ten or eleven that night. He would give speeches and interviews, and meet with citizens on the

REPUBLICANS AND DEMOCRATS

Many different political parties have existed throughout the history of the United States. The two most prominent today, however, are the Republicans and the Democrats. They differ in their basic view of how the nation should be run. The Republicans, for example, generally believe in fewer government programs, lower taxes, conservative social policies, a stronger military, supporting the interests of large businesses, and an active foreign policy. Democrats, on the other hand, usually want a larger government with more programs, higher taxes (to fund those programs), greater emphasis on domestic issues, liberal social policies, and favoritism toward workers.

street or in their homes. Kennedy lost so much weight that he looked like a strong breeze might blow him away. Meanwhile, Joe Sr. spent a fortune on advertising to make sure that everyone in the Eleventh District knew his son's name and face.

In the end, the hard work and sacrifice paid off—on the night of the primary election, Kennedy defeated Mike Neville for the Democratic nomination. Then, on November 5, 1946, Kennedy beat his Republican challenger, Lester Bowen, by almost three times as many votes—69,093 to Bowen's 26,007. He was on his way to the nation's capital to become a member of the U.S. Congress.

The Independent Thinker

Kennedy began his first term in the House of Representatives in January 1947 and quickly began to develop a reputation as an independent thinker. This independence of thought extended to his father, with whom he didn't agree on all political matters. Jack once said, "I've given up arguing with him. I make up my own mind and my own decisions." There were times when he would support ideas from the leaders of his Democratic Party, and days when he would not.

Congressman Kennedy was known as an independent thinker.

The Democrats were known, for example, for their tax-and-spend strategies, which meant taxing the American public at rates higher than the Republicans would have, and using the money for government programs. Kennedy, however, was fairly conservative when it came to money, and he often found himself at odds with Democratic leaders on how much the government should really be spending. The role of government had become larger in the lives of ordinary people during the Great Depression because Franklin Roosevelt's New Deal programs were designed to help people simply survive. But when the Great Depression ended, many of the New Deal programs didn't—and suddenly the government became a kind of support system for many people. Kennedy believed this was dangerous. He feared that overspending would damage the government's effectiveness in the long run.

Kennedy also didn't like the way Democrats often wasted money on programs of relatively low priority. He thought housing and education were very important, and that the government needed to devote more funding to those areas. Many Americans who returned from World War II, for example, were in need of homes, and the new congressman believed that they deserved the government's assistance. Many of America's schools also needed improvement, and Kennedy saw this as a worthwhile investment—better education led to better citizens, and better citizens formed a stronger nation.

When Kennedy sided with the Republicans to add the Twenty-second Amendment to the U.S. Constitution, some Democrats were outraged and nearly called him a traitor. The proposed amendment would limit a president to two terms in office (for a total of eight years). The amendment reflected the concern of many about dire possibilities if another person should, like Franklin Delano Roosevelt, be elected to *four* consecutive terms. Kennedy may have supported the amendment as a result of personal disagreements with Roosevelt on some of the president's important decisions. For example, he thought Roosevelt had given in to too many of the demands of Soviet leader Joseph Stalin during World War II negotiations over the postwar fate of certain European countries. Nevertheless, Kennedy was criticized by fellow Democrats for standing with the Republicans on the Twenty-second Amendment, which was added to the Constitution in 1951.

But Kennedy did side with his party on many other issues. For example, Republicans traditionally protected the interests of employers. Workers, however, often formed groups called unions to fight against unfair labor practices such as overtime hours without extra pay, dangerous working conditions, low wages, and few or no fringe benefits. Kennedy supported the unions to make sure business owners didn't take advantage of their employees. In this respect, he was staying faithful not only to the Democratic Party's basic beliefs but also to the voters in the Massachusetts district he had been elected to represent in Washington.

Kennedy also supported Harry Truman—who as Roosevelt's vice president had become the nation's leader when Roosevelt died in April 1945. Kennedy believed Truman was right to help rebuild and strengthen Europe following World War II; he also favored the Truman Doctrine, according to which the United States sent military and financial aid to the nations of Turkey and Greece to enable them to resist being taken over by the Soviet Union. Soviet leader Joseph Stalin believed in the political philosophy of **communism**. Under communism, the government owned and controlled virtually everything in society, and a citizen's personal freedoms were severely limited. This was in direct contrast to American democracy, where people have much greater freedom of individual choice because government officials know they can be voted out of office.

Although America had fought alongside the Soviet Union in the war against Germany, Japan, and Italy, there was now a tense, distrustful relationship between the two countries. The American-Soviet relationship had degenerated into a conflict over ideologies that became known as the **cold war**. Truman feared that Stalin would try to exploit the weaknesses of war-torn Europe. Stalin might, for example, try to conquer parts of Europe as a kind of payment for the Soviet Union's heavy losses in World War II. So Truman implemented the Marshall Plan, which provided for the rebuilding of many European nations. This way they would regain enough strength to credibly stand up to Stalin's forces.

President Kennedy agreed wholeheartedly with Truman on these measures and spoke in support of them on many occasions. Kennedy thought communism was one of the

A shipment of sugar sent under the Marshall Plan arrives at London's Royal Victoria docks.

greatest threats to freedom the world had ever known, and he would fight many battles against it in the years ahead.

Moving On

Kennedy became so popular in his home state of Massachusetts that he was reelected to two more terms in the House of Representatives, for a total period of three terms in six years. Yet he had grown weary of the position and was ready to move on. It is doubtful that he ever considered his service in the House to be much more than one step on the ladder of professional politics. In many ways, it didn't suit him on a personal scene. First, there was little a representative could do to distinguish himself on the national level. Second, the House was loaded with rules and traditions, and Kennedy was too free-spirited to be comfortable in such a rigid system. And third, he came to see the demands of his constituents as so tedious and tiresome that he hired a large staff to deal with the petitioners so he wouldn't have to.

His time in the House was useful, however. He gained plenty of insight into the ways things worked in Washington, which would certainly be valuable in the years ahead. He later admitted that he didn't know much when he arrived there in 1947: "I wasn't equipped for the job. I didn't plan to get into it, and when I started out as a Congressman, there were lots of things I didn't know, a lot of mistakes I made." He had also raised his national profile by taking part in several congressional committees that dealt with issues affecting people all across the country. One was the House Education and Labor Committee, where he participated in matters concerning both school systems and workers' rights. He also sat on the Veterans' Affairs Committee, fighting for the rights of soldiers returning home from World War II. His father also spent time, money, and energy creating a public image of Kennedy as a rising star in politics, a man on his way to bigger things.

Kennedy also knew that any chance of reaching a higher political office required a reputation for experience in foreign affairs. Privately, he knew his expertise in this area was already considerable. But he had to make sure potential voters knew it, too. So, in the fall of 1951, he undertook an extensive trip abroad, spending nearly two months visiting nine countries in Asia and the Middle East. He talked to hundreds of people, from politicians to ordinary citizens. When he returned, he shared his findings with the public. He talked about the impact American policy was having overseas, and what the future might hold for America's relationship with these countries. Those who listened were impressed with the serious young man—who didn't seem so much like a kid anymore.

ANOTHER TOUGH CAMPAIGN

By the early 1950s Kennedy had a decision to make—which higher political office would be best? He thought about returning to Massachusetts and running for governor, but that position wasn't without limitations. In spite of the overwhelming Democratic strength in Kennedy's congressional district, Republicans had power elsewhere the state. That meant the governor would have to spend valuable time battling with Massachusetts Republicans to get his programs enacted.

A senatorial position was more attractive. As senator, for example, he would play a role in both domestic and foreign affairs. Kennedy believed the two Massachusetts senators who were up for reelection in 1952 could, with a smart and hard-fought campaign, be beaten. The senator in question was Henry Cabot Lodge Jr., a Republican who had already served three terms. He was fairly popular and had strong connections both in Washington and in Massachusetts, so winning the race wouldn't be easy. But Kennedy wanted the job, so he welcomed the fight.

One of his biggest obstacles was his relative lack of experience. Three terms in the House of Representatives, with a record that was hardly distinguished, put him well behind Lodge, who was first elected to the **Senate** in 1936 and knew the job well. Moreover, Kennedy's war record was matched by his opponent. In 1944 Lodge had resigned his Senate seat to take part in World War II; the first U.S. senator to do so since the Civil War. Lodge also shared many of Kennedy's political views, making it difficult for Kennedy to develop a separate identity.

In the end, however, it would be Kennedy's likable personality, good looks, powerful family connections, and freshness that carried the day. With growing charisma, he spoke about disciplined government spending, workers' rights, improved education, and the fight against the spread of communism. Kennedy's family also got involved—his father spent millions in advertising, while his mother and sisters held public tea parties, inviting local women to listen to Kennedy speak, ask him questions, and meet him afterward. Kennedy's brother Robert F. Kennedy, who was more than eight years younger, became the campaign's manager at the request of Joe Sr. In spite of having no such experience, Bobby worked tirelessly, displaying exceptional organizational skills as well as his father's tenacity, to get Jack elected. Sometimes the younger man's gung-ho attitude irritated people, but he didn't care.

Kennedy is surrounded by his brother and sisters as they work together on his 1952 senate campaign.

"They don't have to like me," Bobby confided to a friend at the time. "I only want them to like Jack."

On election night, in November 1952, Kennedy eked out a victory against Lodge by just under 71,000 votes. This was a tiny margin compared with the 2.35 million total votes that were cast. But it was still impressive, since Republicans swept elections elsewhere across the nation—including the presidential race, in which World War II hero Dwight D. Eisenhower easily defeated his Democratic opponent Adlai Stevenson. Kennedy's victory was considered to be an upset by most. But, upset or not, John F. Kennedy was now part of an exclusive club that had only ninety-six members—the U.S. Senate.

THE U.S. SENATE . . . AND BEYOND

Senator Kennedy quickly gained a reputation among his staff as a man with tremendous energy and plenty of ideas. He would often burst into the office early in the morning and rattle off orders, or call at strange hours while traveling. His aides and secretaries sometimes found his erratic habits exasperating—as in his school days, he didn't have much sense of organization or time. But his passion for the job was tremendous, and the people who worked with him were very loyal. Kennedy also insisted that all requests from the Massachusetts voters—whether they came as letters, phone calls, or personal visits—be dealt with promptly and efficiently. He and his staff worked long days—so long, in fact, that fellow senator Barry Goldwater once remarked that Kennedy's office was the only one still busy when he left at night.

In spite of the ambitious work schedule Kennedy set for himself, he found time for romance—shortly before he became a senator in 1951, he met a woman named Jacqueline Bouvier at a dinner party. Bouvier was slender, dark-haired, and strikingly beautiful. Like Kennedy, she came from a wealthy and privileged family. She was also well educated, tough in mind and spirit, and had a love for writing and reading. Although the two got along well on that first occasion, they were too busy in their separate lives to build a serious relationship. But they stayed in touch through letters and phone calls, and they grew closer around the time Kennedy was running for the Senate. Bouvier attended several of the famous tea parties during the campaign, and she was his date at the party for his senatorial inauguration in January 1953. That June, the couple announced their engagement, and they were married on September 12.

Back at the office, Kennedy's reputation for independent thinking continued to grow. He often found himself caught between wanting to do what was best for Massachusetts versus choosing the best course for America overall. To help his state, he made a diligent effort to improve the sagging Massachusetts economy. Massachusetts had lost millions because of businesses

FRENCH HERITAGE

Jacqueline Bouvier Kennedy was very proud of her French heritage, which played an important role throughout her life. In her junior year of college, she attended the prestigious Sorbonne in Paris, where she became fluent in French, a language she had heard since childhood. Upon her return to the United States the following year, she received a degree from George Washington University in French literature. In later years, after her husband became president, Jackie traveled to France several times and was enormously popular there. Once on a state visit to France, Jack introduced himself as Jackie's husband—a little joke that drew enthusiastic applause from the audience.

Senator John F. Kennedy and Jacqueline Bouvier were married September 12, 1953.

that either failed or left the state to find cheaper labor elsewhere. With these losses came financial struggles in other parts of New England, as well. So Kennedy got together with economic advisers and other senators—including several Republicans—and came up with a detailed plan to help important Massachusetts industries through tax breaks, new government contracts, and other incentives. The plan didn't stimulate the New England economy as much as Kennedy would've liked, but it demonstrated that he was trying his best. He was also following his belief that a strong Massachusetts made for a stronger America overall.

On the other hand, in early 1954 he had to make a decision on a matter that would benefit the country as a whole but probably would hurt businesses in Massachusetts and elsewhere in New England. The proposed St. Lawrence Seaway Project was aimed at creating a new waterway that ran farther into mainland America and Canada than any other. It would give many industries access to shipping lanes that they presently couldn't use. For textile manufacturers in Massachusetts, however, this potential influx of shippers meant more competition (and, as a result, smaller profits).

Kennedy agonized over his position on the St. Lawrence issue, but in the end he decided to vote for the project because it would help his country more than it would hurt his home state. The St. Lawrence Seaway became a huge success, and the backlash from Massachusetts wasn't as bad as Kennedy had expected. Also, the vote established him as a man who was willing to stand up for what he felt was right even if it was unpopular among his constituents. Kennedy had decided he would neither sell himself to special-interest groups nor make any decision based on

A cargo ship sails on the St. Lawrence Seaway, a project that Kennedy supported as senator.

whether it would affect his chances of getting reelected. He saw such self-interest and short-sightedness in other senators and was alarmed by it. Once, when asked what it was like being a U.S. senator, he replied, "It's the most corrupting job in the world."

PROBLEMS IN ASIA

In 1950 fighting had broken out in the peninsular Asian nation of Korea. Both U.S. and Soviet forces had occupied the area during World War II, but they couldn't agree on who would govern Korea when the war ended. Ultimately they decided to divide the nation into two parts—north and south. The communist Soviet leadership would rule North Korea, and America's democratic leadership would rule South Korea. The arrangement was supposed to be temporary, with the idea that Korea would soon be reunified under a government acceptable to all the people. In June 1950, however, North Korean forces attacked South Korea, and a prolonged conflict ensued. Although the communists had hoped to prevail, thus gaining control of both halves of the country, the Korean War ended in 1953 with a truce but no clear victor. Korea remains divided to this day.

A similar problem developed elsewhere in the former French colony of Indochina. During World War II, much of the region, which included present-day Vietnam, was occupied and controlled by the Japanese. When Japan surrendered in 1945, French leaders wanted the colony to return to their control. They set up a puppet government in the south, but a nationalist political activist in the north had different ideas: Ho Chi Minh was a communist who said he wanted his people to be independent rather than under the control of any colonial power. He quickly formed a government and raised an army.

French military forces, with help from America as well as Vietnamese people who didn't

Ho Chi Minh led northern Vietnam to be an independent communist region after World War II.

want to live under communist rule, tried to regain control from Ho Chi Minh. But the armies of the North proved tougher than anyone had expected, and in 1954 the French were defeated militarily. It was then decided that Vietnam, like Korea, would be temporarily divided into a northern and a southern republic.

While North Vietnam had been governed since 1945 by Ho Chi Minh, South Vietnam followed a different path, coming in 1954 under the rule of its former prime minister, Ngo Dinh Diem. U.S. president Dwight Eisenhower was comfortable having Diem in control of South Vietnam—Diem was against communism and at first seemed happy to follow American directives. Eisenhower's approach to the new problem of the spread of communism was to contain it—to make sure it didn't gain any more strength around the world than it already had. To help Diem in Vietnam, he sent money, military equipment, and advisers to train the army. The ultimate goal, however, was political: the Americans wanted Diem to win the election of 1956 and, eventually to assume control of both parts of Vietnam. But the projected elections never took place, and problems began to develop between the United States and the puppet government in South Vietnam.

Weak Body, Strong Mind

In spite of Kennedy's senatorial successes and his new marriage, the specter of poor health lingered. His back, in particular, was causing almost constant pain. Not long into his new job, he began using crutches. In Senate chambers, they steadied him as he stood to give speeches. Eventually the pain became so intense that he was forced to voice his opinions while sitting down. These physical limitations frustrated and infuriated Kennedy to the point of opting for an operation so risky that it was opposed by family and friends alike. Referring to the crutches, he said, "I'd rather die than spend the rest of my life on these things."

He had the operation on October 21, 1954, in New York. Although the procedure itself went relatively smoothly, Kennedy developed a serious infection on the third day of recovery that almost ended his life. He became so gravely ill, in fact, that he

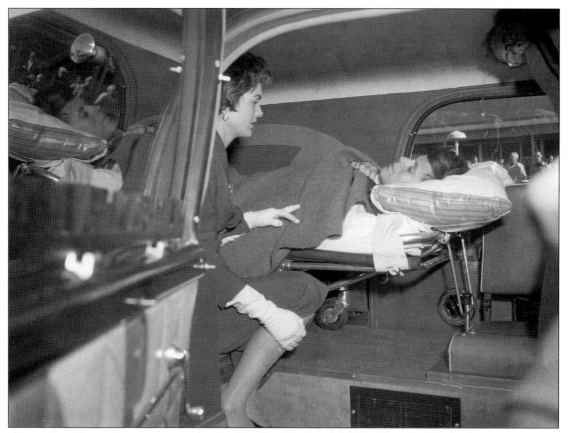

Jacqueline Kennedy accompanies her husband to the family's Palm Beach, Florida, home to recuperate after surgery.

received the **last rites** of the Roman Catholic Church. Neverthe-less, his condition improved, and he left the hospital shortly before Christmas to recuperate at the Kennedy family's house in warm and sunny Palm Beach, Florida. He had to return to New York for a follow-up operation in February but was soon back in Florida, where he would remain until early May, attended by several nurses and by his wife. When his spirits were low, Jackie would play games with him, read aloud, and invite friends over.

One other bright spot during Kennedy's recovery period was an explosion of personal creativity—while almost completely bedridden, he undertook a book project. With the help of several friends and research assistants, he compiled eight stories of past senators who, while serving in Congress, had stood by their con-victions and done what they felt was right even if it hurt their careers. Kennedy thought the book's theme was crucial at a time when many of his colleagues on Capital Hill were abandoning their principles, whether yielding to special-interest groups with money and influence or to political peers who pressured them to follow the crowd and not rock the boat, or because they wanted to make sure they got reelected. Kennedy's daughter, Caroline, would later write that her father "believed that telling the stories of those who act on principle regardless of cost can help inspire future generations to follow their example." The book, entitled *Profiles in Courage*, was released on New Year's Day, 1956, and was an immediate hit with both critics and the public. In an age when political integrity seemed to be diminishing, Kennedy was applauded for drawing attention to examples of it. The book also increased people's confidence in his own integrity—which further improved his image nationwide.

Senator Kennedy signs copies of Profiles in Courage *after its publication in 1956.*

VICE PRESIDENT . . . ALMOST

In early 1956, with a presidential election coming in November, Kennedy saw an opportunity to further his political career by taking a shot at the nomination for the vice presidency. President Eisenhower, a Republican, had been enormously popular with the American people during his first term, which began in 1952. But it wasn't certain that he would run again in 1956 because he had suffered a massive heart attack in September 1955. Seeing an opportunity to win back the White House, the Democrats chose popular Illinois governor Adlai Stevenson to be their presidential election nominee. Several prominent Democrats hoped to be Stevenson's running mate—and Kennedy was one of them.

Many of Kennedy's closest friends and advisers—including his father—thought this was a bad idea. They said his career would essentially be over if he got the nomination and he and Stevenson lost—it was tough enough for a presidential candidate to continue his career with a reputation as a loser, but it was nearly impossible for the running mate. Also, Kennedy risked making enemies within his own party because he'd have to fight for the spot, a spot that had few responsibilities and little power. The Constitution directs that the vice president preside over the Senate, and that he assume executive power should the president become incapacitated or die. And, by tradition, the vice president supports the president's positions regardless of whether he agrees with them. Not exactly an office in which a young and ambitious politician like Jack Kennedy would be able to shine.

But he asked for the nomination anyway, and Adlai Stevenson gave the request serious consideration. The two men shared the same views on many issues, and Kennedy's charisma would certainly attract voters to a ticket headed by the scholarly governor. Also Stevenson had been divorced from his wife of twenty-one years, which some voters didn't like—and Kennedy, in his happy new marriage to Jackie, would ease some of that disapproval.

In the end, however, Stevenson decided to put the choice in the hands of the delegates at the Democratic National Convention. Each major political party holds a convention every four years, usually in the summer before the general election, to establish their policies going forward and to officially choose their candidates for president and vice president. Kennedy did well in this small internal election, but in the end he came in second to Tennessee senator Estes Kefauver. After the loss, Kennedy gave a stirring and gracious speech. As a result, he impressed millions of Americans across the nation. He also

Kennedy speaks at the 1956 Democratic National Convention.

avoided a huge disaster—Eisenhower did run for a second term, and he crushed the Stevenson/Kefauver ticket in a landslide.

Kennedy returned to his senatorial duties, and 1957 brought him two wonderful moments. In May, *Profiles in Courage* received one of the most coveted and respected literary awards in the world, the Pulitzer Prize for biographies. Then, on November 27, the senator and his wife celebrated the birth of their first child, a daughter they named Caroline Bouvier. It is also likely that 1957 was the year in which Kennedy finally decided to commit himself fully to his ultimate dream in professional politics—becoming president. And he knew that to do this, he would first have to position himself on several key issues of foreign and domestic policy.

As a new member of the Senate Foreign Relations Committee, Kennedy took part in debates about the growing cold war tension between America and the Soviet Union, and about the degree to which America should get involved in the conflict between France and the rising nationalist faction in Vietnam. A larger foreign policy issue—and one that would be linked to both the cold war and the Southeast Asia problem—was the threat of communism spreading to the American homeland. Ever since the end of World War II, which left the Soviet Union with tremendous power, Americans had worried that communists would eventually work their way into all sectors of American society. Kennedy, who had always been vigorously anticommunist, assured the public that he would fight off any threats from that direction.

On domestic issues, Kennedy knew he would have little chance of reaching the presidency without supporting the civil rights movement: the budding attempt by blacks and other

Senator Kennedy and wife Jacqueline with baby Caroline in 1958.

minorities to obtain fair and equal treatment in all areas of American life. Kennedy had never opposed the movement, yet previously he had had no political stance on it one way or the other. He needed one now, however, as black votes could swing a presidential election in his favor. Even so, he had to be very careful about upsetting members of his own political party, whose support he also needed—Democrats in the southern states were not as open-minded about civil rights as those in the North. If Kennedy supported the civil rights movement, he would lose many votes in the South. If he didn't support it, he'd lose votes in the North.

Workers' rights were another important domestic issue. While Kennedy had played a role in helping to strengthen unions, he and others had also unintentionally contributed to a new problem—some union leaders, entrusted with members' money and empowered as elected officeholders, became corrupt. They stole from union accounts for personal gain and bullied union members to suit their own purposes. Kennedy helped to pass new laws against this kind of corruption, further endearing himself to ordinary American workers.

NOMINATION

Convincing voters that he was the right man for the job was one thing. Convincing his fellow Democrats was another, and leading Democrats weren't certain Kennedy was the best choice for the 1960 race. First of all, there was his age—if he ran, he would try to be the youngest president in U.S. history. Many felt voters would equate youth with lack of experience. Then there was his Roman Catholic religion (also a presidential first). Only once in

American history had a Catholic been nominated for the presidency—Al Smith, a Democrat, who was beaten decisively in the 1928 election by Republican Herbert Hoover. Some Democrats worried that Kennedy would be too strongly influenced by leaders of his church, potentially violating the American tradition of separation of church and state. And in spite of Kennedy's efforts to walk a fine line on the civil rights issue, he hadn't developed much popularity in the South—yet without the southern states, he'd never make it to the White House.

THE YOUNGEST PRESIDENT EVER ELECTED— BUT NOT THE YOUNGEST EVER

In 1960 John F. Kennedy would become the youngest man elected to the American presidency—but he would not be the youngest to hold the office. In September 1901 President William McKinley was assassinated while attending a world's fair in Buffalo, New York. Upon McKinley's death, the presidency was automatically passed to his vice president, Theodore Roosevelt. Roosevelt was forty-two at the time, whereas Kennedy was forty-three when he won the election in 1960. Bill Clinton was forty-six when he beat sitting president George H. W. Bush in November 1992. Barack Obama was forty-seven when he won over John McCain in 2008.

In spite of all these concerns, Kennedy forged ahead. He formally announced his presidential candidacy on January 2, 1960. Backed by generous contributions from supporters as well as from his father, he followed the same strategy that got him elected first to the House and then to the Senate—he went out and met ordinary Americans face to face. While his opponents for the nomination were attacking him, he was shaking hands and making speeches. Meanwhile, the rest of his family also got involved—Bobby ran the campaign, while the other Kennedys made contact with as many potential voters as possible. Kennedy struggled with ongoing pain from his many health issues, but he refused to let it show. There were times when he would lie in the backseat of a car, fists clenched and teeth gritted in agony, then hop out with a smile and greet people as if he felt wonderful.

In July, with Kennedy's national popularity sailing at new highs, the Democratic Party had little choice but to nominate him as their presidential candidate at the convention in Los Angeles. At this time, Kennedy would formally announce his choice for running mate—Lyndon Baines Johnson. Like Kennedy, Johnson had been a member of the House before joining the Senate. He was a tall, gregarious individual with tremendous political skills and, as a Texan, would help Kennedy carry the crucial southern states where the Massachusetts native was weak.

KENNEDY VS. NIXON

Now Kennedy faced one last hurdle before reaching the White House—Republican candidate Richard M. Nixon had been vice president under Eisenhower for both terms. Before that he had

Senator Kennedy shakes hands with supporters while on the presidential campaign trail in 1960.

A campaign button announces John F. Kennedy and his vice-presidential running mate, Lyndon B. Johnson.

been, like Kennedy and Johnson, a member of the House of Representatives and then of the Senate. Nixon was a skilled politician and an excellent public speaker. His rhetorical skills had been very much on display in September 1952 when, in response to accusations of having accepted a large illegal donation, he went on national television to make a case for his innocence. The speech was so well written and delivered that Nixon received the public's overwhelming support, and the scandal never went any further. With eight years of experience as vice president, Nixon more than matched Kennedy in knowledge of foreign affairs. All in all, Nixon was a formidable opponent.

The race was close throughout the campaign, with Nixon showing a slight lead at the beginning. In spite of the obvious stress of being behind, Kennedy often handled the situation with characteristic good humor. While giving a speech in Flint, Michigan, he said, "I don't see how the Flint High School football team ever loses any football game with that cheering section. If they are not busy for the next two months in school, we will be glad to take them with us all around the United States." Nevertheless, early polls suggested that people felt Nixon's time as vice president gave him an edge over Kennedy as far as experience was

Kennedy's opponent during the 1960 presidential campaign was Richard M. Nixon, a well-polished and experienced politician.

concerned. Nixon was also adept at manipulating fears about the spread of communism—a significant issue in the minds of many American voters. Nixon also benefited from continuing concerns over Kennedy's health, and his religion, and his youth. Nixon was, in fact, only a few years older—but he came across as more mature and statesmanlike, whereas Kennedy still gave the impression of being quite young.

But Kennedy, having devoted so much of his adult life to pursuing the dream of reaching the White House, had no intention of being beaten. He attacked Nixon on every front. For example, he berated Nixon and Eisenhower for economic difficulties—during their administration, he pointed out, the economic growth maintained by Democratic presidents since the 1940s had slowed considerably. He also challenged Nixon at his own game of creating fear of communism by saying that Nixon and Eisenhower had failed to keep up with the Soviet Union in terms of building military power, leaving America vulnerable.

KENNEDY GETS SOME UNEXPECTED HELP

In a surprising moment during the 1960 campaign, Kennedy got help from, of all people, President Eisenhower. When Eisenhower was asked by a reporter what ideas of Nixon's he had used during his eight years in office, Eisenhower replied, "If you give me a week, I might think of one." Although Eisenhower later said he was joking, the remark undoubtedly hurt Nixon's image as a key player in Eisenhower's administration.

By early fall of 1960 the race was too close to call. Then, in late September, Kennedy and Nixon appeared in the first-ever televised debate between presidential candidates. The two men discussed all the major issues of the day, and in this respect they were evenly matched. Both displayed great poise, knowledge, and passion, suggesting that either would make a fine president. But it was their physical appearance that made the difference—Nixon looked pale and haggard, having lost weight after a recent two-week hospital stay. He perspired under the hot lights, and his clothes didn't seem to fit him well. Kennedy, on the other hand, was smooth and relaxed, breezing through his answers with ease and confidence. He smiled, made jokes, and came across as everyone's friend. Most importantly, however, he seemed *presidential*. Those who listened to the debates on the radio felt the debate had been a tie—but those who watched on television declared Kennedy the winner.

In early November, the voters agreed—John Fitzgerald Kennedy beat Richard Nixon to become the thirty-fifth president of the United States. Although he had easily scored enough electoral votes—303 to Nixon's 219—the difference in terms of popular votes was among the smallest in American history—just over 118,000 votes out of a total 68.8 million. Nevertheless, Kennedy had achieved his cherished dream. And for more good news in the same month, Jackie had another baby—on November 25, John F. Kennedy Jr. was born. The growing Kennedy family was moving to the White House.

PRESIDENT KENNEDY'S DOMESTIC POLICIES

Five

On January 20, 1961, John F. Kennedy was sworn in as the thirty-fifth president of the United States. Standing on the steps of the Capitol, he gave one of the most famous speeches in American history. He spoke of friendships with other nations while giving warnings to those who chose to be adversaries instead. He suggested that a country as powerful as America

President Kennedy delivers his inaugural speech at the Capitol on January 20, 1961.

should devote itself to achieving great things, and he stated that freedom was the birthright of all people everywhere. Then, toward the end, he delivered one of the most unforgettable lines spoken by an American president, "And so, my fellow Americans, ask not what your country can do for you—ask what you can do for your country." His energy, his youth, and his hopes set the tone for what many believed would be an administration full of new and exciting ideas both at home and abroad.

THE SPACE RACE

In April 1961 the Soviet Union made a startling announcement—they had sent a man into space and safely returned him to Earth. Both the Soviet Union and America had been working on space exploration programs, and the competition to see who would be the first to make a major breakthrough was known as the space race. With the news of Soviet cosmonaut Yuri Gagarin's successful orbit around the planet, the communist nation declared itself the winner with respect to this important first step.

President Eisenhower had authorized the creation of the National Aeronautics and Space Administration (NASA) in 1958, and Kennedy, now alarmed by the Soviets' progress, decided that keeping up with the Soviets called for the expansion of NASA. He was particularly resentful of the way the Soviets bragged about Gagarin's journey as a cold war "victory," that is, proof that the communist system was superior to democracy.

Kennedy persuaded Congress to commit billions of dollars to an improved space program, and by May NASA had also successfully sent a man into space. In February 1962 Lieutenant Colonel John Glenn matched Gagarin's achievement by orbiting the earth and returning alive. Kennedy didn't want to keep up with the Soviets however he wanted to surpass them. He had told

Congress in May 1961—"I believe that this nation should commit itself to achieving the goal, before this decade is out, of landing a man on the moon and returning him safely to the Earth."

This ambitious vision became a reality in July 1969 when *Apollo 11* carried astronauts Neil Armstrong and Edwin "Buzz" Aldrin to the moon. They fulfilled Kennedy's dream by walking on the moon's surface and then returning home four days later. The Soviet space program, on the other hand, had become bogged down in inefficiency and internal fighting, and the communist nation had fallen far behind America by the end of the 1960s.

Astronaut Edwin "Buzz" Aldrin is photographed on the Moon beside the American flag in July 1969.

Struggles with the Economy and Big Business

When Kennedy became president, America was in the middle of a mild economic recession, a period of diminished growth that affected everything from the prices of ordinary products and services to the stability of the businesses that provided people's jobs. After discussing the problem with his economic advisers, Kennedy came up with a plan to get America's economy growing again.

Leaders in the business community had never been big supporters of President Kennedy. They were Republicans for the most part, and their party usually looked more favorably than Democrats upon businesses. Business leaders also remembered the way Kennedy had fought for the interests of labor, rather than management, during his time in the House and Senate. Nevertheless, Kennedy knew he had to help both businesses and their employees if the economy was going to thrive.

One part of Kennedy's plan that business leaders did like was tax breaks. The president knew that many American businesses were using outdated equipment and operating in buildings that were badly in need of repair or modernization. To encourage such companies to invest some of their profits in improving their facilities and equipment, he urged Congress to reduce the taxes of firms that took these steps. Kennedy also worked to make it easier for American businesses to sell their products overseas, creating opportunities to make greater profits.

Slowly, the business community began changing its mind about Kennedy—for awhile. Then came an incident that brought this to a halt. It began in the steel manufacturing business in March 1962, when the Kennedy administration worked with labor and management to reach an agreement designed to give both parties what they wanted—or, at least, to get them both to the point where they'd be content. Kennedy was pleased with the collective bargaining agreement that had been created in the steel industry—the workers would receive pay raises, but not in amounts that would force the businesses to increase their prices.

Not long after this agreement was reached, however, the business leaders in the steel industry increased their prices anyway. Infuriated, President Kennedy demanded proof that the price increase had been necessary. In the end, the steelmakers dropped their prices again—but Kennedy was labeled an antibusiness president. This upset Kennedy because he needed support from the business community for other parts of his economic plan. In the end, the American economy did enjoy some growth, but not as much as Kennedy had hoped.

Kennedy had additional successes in labor relations, as well. In 1961 he secured an increase in the minimum wage, and in 1963 he signed the Equal Pay Act, which made it illegal for businesses to give women less money than men for the same work. He formed the Equal Employment Opportunity Commission to combat race discrimination in businesses that received contracts from the government. He also created a program to help workers develop new skills if they lost jobs as a result of emerging technologies.

CIVIL RIGHTS

Kennedy's position on civil rights had, for many years, been difficult to pinpoint. While he was a lifelong Democrat—the party that had, in the twentieth century, given more support to civil rights—Kennedy's record on the issue was spotty at best. As someone who had known only wealth and privilege, he'd had little interaction with minorities, so it was hard for many to imagine that he would truly care about the average black American.

Nevertheless, once Kennedy became president, spokesmen for the civil rights movement, led most notably by Dr. Martin Luther King Jr., were expecting him to help them. King publicly called for Kennedy to use all the powers of his office to bring about the passage of new laws ensuring that black Americans would be treated fairly and equally. There were already laws against segregation, but they weren't being honored everywhere. King and his followers wanted Kennedy to make sure they were properly enforced.

Whatever Kennedy's feelings were on the civil rights issue, he had little choice but to act shortly after taking office. In May 1961 a group of thirteen civil rights activists—six whites and seven blacks—set out on a bus trip from Washington, D.C., to New Orleans. Calling themselves the Freedom Riders, they planned to demonstrate that antisegregation laws were being ignored in certain parts of America. They purposely entered restaurants, restrooms, and other areas marked "Whites Only," to test the public reaction. In the early part of the journey, they encountered no trouble of note. Once in the Deep South, however, things got rough. Ordinary citizens in Alabama cursed at them, beat them, hurled rocks and bottles, and set their bus on fire. More Freedom Riders entered the area in new buses, and they expanded the trip into Mississippi. Eventually, Kennedy's brother Bobby, who had been appointed attorney general of the United States, sent four hundred federal marshals to protect the Freedom Riders from further harm. When the Riders were arrested and jailed in Mississippi, Bobby Kennedy offered to have them released. Martin Luther King Jr. declined the offer, reasoning that the civil rights

U.S. National Guardsmen protect the civil rights activists known as the "Freedom Riders" as they make their way to New Orleans.

workers were making a stronger statement for the cause by remaining imprisoned. In the end, although a majority of Americans believed that the Freedom Riders were troublemakers, the Kennedy administration's actions to ensure their safety met with general approval.

Kennedy's second major civil rights crisis occurred in September 1962. Some ten months previously, a black man named James Meredith had applied for admission at the University of Mississippi in Oxford. This particular branch of the university had only white students, but Meredith, inspired by the new antisegregationist laws concerning educational facilities, decided to apply anyway. When his application was denied, he fought the school in court and in 1962, a judge ruled that the Oxford branch had to let him in.

Nevertheless, school officials, led by Mississippi governor Ross Barnett, refused. Kennedy and his brother then ordered marshals into the area to see that Meredith was allowed to complete his registration, to settle into his dormitory, and to stay there unharmed. To the Kennedys' surprise, thousands of angry Mississippians converged upon the area, sparking violence and rioting that lasted several days. Ultimately, over 20,000 troops were sent in to restore and maintain order, and Meredith began attending classes. But two people were killed in the fighting, and almost four hundred more were injured.

James Meredith had to endure a jeering crowd after registering for classes at the University of Mississippi in 1962.

In spite of Kennedy's willingness to take action against those who ignored antisegregationist laws, many civil rights leaders remained disappointed that he wasn't doing more. As Kennedy biographer Thomas C. Reeves noted, "[Kennedy] took some modest steps early in the administration to implement some of the civil rights promises made by Democrats during the campaign. But his actions were sharply limited." Realizing that this was a problem that needed serious solutions, Kennedy appointed more than forty blacks to important government posts—exceeding the record of any other president up to that point. He also made an impassioned speech in June 1963 stating that it was time for a broad-based set of rules to advance the interests of black Americans. This led to the creation of a civil rights act that among other things, outlawed discrimination in public places, gave the government power to take action against schools and business, and protected the rights of black voters. Although Kennedy's proposal went through several changes and adjustments in Congress, becoming law in July 1964—a triumph the president would not live to see.

LIFE IN THE KENNEDY WHITE HOUSE

Kennedy created a relaxed atmosphere inside the White House. Staff members recall the president going out of his way to learn everyone's name and treat each of them like an ordinary person rather than as a servant. He spent time each day either in the White House gym or in the swimming pool. His doctors had given him a set of exercises to strengthen his back and reduce the pain, and the swimming, as long as the water was warm enough, was particularly effective. He would also take short naps, usually in the early afternoon, to recharge his batteries so that he could work late into the night.

One of Jackie Kennedy's main contributions to the White House was a dramatic improvement of its appearance. It had seen so many decorative changes over the years that it had become a mix of styles. Jackie decided to bring it back to its original elegance. She personally chose appropriate furnishings, fixtures, paint, wallpaper, and so on. When she ran out of the money allotted for the project, she raised more by creating the White House Historical Association, which could receive donations from ordinary citizens. She also oversaw the publication of a book called *The White House: An Historical Guide*, which became a best seller. In February 1962, by means of a television program that was watched by more than 40 million viewers, she invited the American public on a tour of the fully restored White House.

Even though both led busy lives, the president and his wife were caring and attentive parents. Jackie was highly protective of her children, wanting them to lead reasonably normal lives rather than be the focus of media attention. The president always made time to sit and talk with them, and he would often arrive in the Oval Office in the morning holding their hands. John Jr. liked to hide inside a secret compartment underneath his father's desk. Occasionally the children were indiscreet—once asked what her father was doing, Caroline answered he was sitting upstairs, "not doing anything." John Jr., for his part, interrupted a radio speech Kennedy was delivering. Overall, however, the young Kennedys were happy and well behaved.

Ongoing health problems comprised one of the few negative aspects of Kennedy's personal life in the White House. In spite of having some of the best doctors available, Kennedy suffered severe back pains, stomach and colon ailments, chronic headaches and fevers, difficulty falling and staying asleep, and

John F. Kennedy Jr. explores a hiding spot under his father's Oval Office desk.

The President Pitches In

While his wife was fixing up the White House on the inside, President Kennedy devoted a little time to improving it on the outside. He took a personal interest in the landscaping, often complaining about brown spots on the lawn or flowers and shrubs that didn't look colorful enough. He eventually brought in a personal friend who was a professional gardener, and together they designed a landscape that would impress visitors and give the White House the kind of feel Kennedy thought it deserved. Once the work was done, his only concern seemed to be making sure his daughter's pony, Macaroni, didn't trample through the flower beds. He would often tell his secretary to go out and shoo the animal away.

adrenal disorders. He took many different medications and couldn't function without them. He struggled through each day with extreme physical discomfort.

Another health-related issue struck Kennedy hard during his presidency, although it happened to someone else—in December 1961, while playing golf in Florida, Joe Kennedy Sr. suffered a massive stroke that left him unable to walk, speak, or care for himself. The president made sure his father received excellent care and visited him as often as possible, but he was heartbroken to see a man once so strong now as weak and helpless as an infant.

PRESIDENT KENNEDY'S FOREIGN POLICIES

*F*oreign policy had always been Kennedy's favorite political subject. He believed that America's relationship with other nations was crucial to its future and that foreign threats to America's security had to be addressed with the utmost seriousness. America shouldn't merely play a role in international affairs, he believed—for better or for worse, it had to be a leader.

THE PEACE CORPS

Before he was president, Kennedy had traveled extensively throughout nations of the world that were underdeveloped in terms of industry and economy, and whose citizens lived in poverty with little hope of improvement. The suffering he had seen alarmed and appalled Kennedy, and he came to the conclusion that America, with all its might, influence, and resources, should do something about it.

In 1960, while campaigning for the presidency, he suggested to a group of students that they might want to devote a year or two of their lives to working in an underdeveloped nation to help impoverished people outside North America to build and strengthen their communities. A medical school graduate, for example, could create and help execute a program to immunize a village against, say, malaria, and then teach the villagers how to avoid the disease in the first place. An engineer could show people how to build better homes, roads, and bridges. And a farmer could pass along new techniques to promote increased crop growth.

Inspired by proposals made by former presidential nominee Adlai Stevenson, Kennedy decided to form an organization to sponsor volunteers for such a program, which he called the Peace Corps. Roosevelt's Depression-era Civilian Conservation Corps probably was another model. Rather than place the new organization in an existing governmental agency—where it might become bogged down in bureaucracy and red tape and therefore end up ineffective—Kennedy made the Peace Corps independent. He then followed its progress closely and supported it by lending his name to projects. He also praised the volunteers in speeches, well aware that they faced enormous challenges. The Peace Corps volunteers had, he once said, "one of the most sensitive and difficult assignments which any administrative group in

A Peace Corps volunteer walks with village children in the African nation of Togo.

The Peace Corps Today

Almost half a century after President Kennedy created the Peace Corps, the organization is still going strong. Nearly 200,000 volunteers have worked in more than 125 countries, sharing technological knowledge, bringing food and medical aid, and making environmental improvements. The average age of a Peace Corps volunteer is twenty-seven, and most volunteers have a college education.

Washington has been given in this century." But the rewards, Kennedy knew, would be well worth the effort.

Thanks to the volunteers' selfless commitment to hard work, Peace Corps accomplish a purpose broader than assistance to any individual community. During the cold war, when America and the Soviet Union were competing for influence around the world, Peace Corps volunteers showed people far from the reach of formal diplomatic initiatives that Americans were generous with their resources, both human and material.

The Alliance for Progress

Early in his presidency, Kennedy decided that more attention needed to be given to growing problems in Latin America: the Spanish-speaking countries in Central and South America, plus the islands of the Caribbean. Latin America had developed a hostile attitude toward the United States for not being more concerned with its problems, which included poor economic prospects, lackluster industrial development, a shortage of reliable schools, and high jobless rates.

In March 1961 Kennedy proposed an ambitious ten-year plan that he called the Alliance for Progress. Its goals, he said, was "to complete the revolution of the Americas, to build a hemisphere where all men can hope for a suitable standard of living and all can live out their lives in dignity and in freedom." He asked Congress to devote billions of dollars to important areas such as education, housing, roadways, hospitals, and sources of energy. These contributions would not only improve the image of the United States in Latin America but would help the benefiting countries understand the value of democracy and **capitalism**—once again, the direct opposite of communism. Kennedy knew that Latin America was vulnerable to the Soviet Union's influence, so he hoped to create new allies through his plan.

The Alliance for Progress seemed to work for a while, then it stalled. Many Latin American countries experienced a population explosion in the 1960s, which increased the strain on their troubled economies. Also, the American government was often slow in providing help when it was needed the most. Worst of all, perhaps, was the success of the Soviet Union in gaining the loyalty of one Latin American leader—Fidel Castro, who in January 1959 had overthrown president Fulgencio Batista. Castro's partnership with the Soviet Union not only made Kennedy nervous, it also made him hesitant to commit more money and attention to other Latin American nations. In the end, the Alliance for Progress fell short of many of its goals, but it did help keep some Latin American leaders from falling under communist influence.

THE BAY OF PIGS

The growing threat of communism occupied a great deal of President Kennedy's thoughts—particularly when he decided to take action against Fidel Castro in what became known as the Bay of Pigs invasion.

When Castro forced Fulgencio Batista out of office and became Cuba's leader, Kennedy and most other Americans supported him. Batista had been a brutal and corrupt dictator who relentlessly oppressed most of the Cuban people. Castro, on the other hand, said he wanted to give Cubans all the personal freedoms enjoyed in America and other Western democracies. Once Castro was in power, however, he forgot these promises—he attacked people who held political views that were different from his, took over many businesses owned by American companies, and formed partnerships with communist leaders in the Soviet Union. The Soviet government gave Castro money, began trading goods and services with Cuba, and—perhaps most alarming to Kennedy—considered using Cuba, only 90 miles from Key West, Florida, as a military base. Castro also assisted others in Latin America who were trying to overthrow their governments and replace them with communist regimes. With all this in mind, Kennedy believed Castro had to go.

President Eisenhower had already approved a secret plan of the Central Intelligence Agency (CIA) to remove Castro from power. He didn't get a chance to carry it out, however, so it was passed to Kennedy. The idea was to train a group of Cuban exiles to invade their homeland and, with the help of Cubans still on the island who felt that Castro had deceived them, topple the new government. The plan took its name from the landing site—an area in southern Cuba known as *Bahía de Chochinos*, the Bay of Pigs.

The invasion, which began on April 15, 1961, with several airplane bombings, quickly turned into a mess. First, word of the plan had leaked long before the operation was set to begin, so Castro and his forces were ready. Second, when the exiles arrived at the Bay of Pigs two days later, they discovered that Castro's army was much stronger and better trained than they had expected. Third, the invasion team experienced one problem after another—radios that didn't work,

In 1963 Life *magazine reported on the unpleasant realities behind the Bay of Pigs invasion.*

mistakes in timing, and equipment lost or destroyed by enemy attacks. Finally, the Cuban people didn't seem to be as interested in overthrowing Castro as Kennedy and others had thought. The invasion came to an embarrassing end just three days after it had begun. Over a hundred died, and more than a thousand were captured and imprisoned.

Kennedy took the defeat personally, and he accepted full responsibility. One biographer wrote that, "the loss of life during the Bay of Pigs invasion brought him to tears." There is strong evidence, however, that the president was given misleading information by his intelligence advisers. Nevertheless, the incident was humiliating for the administration, and both Castro and his Soviet allies made a point of telling the world that it was proof of America's desire to take over smaller, weaker countries. Instead of easing the tension between America and the Soviet Union, the Bay of Pigs disaster made it worse.

KENNEDY AND KHRUSHCHEV

Kennedy knew that the tension between the world's two super-powers had to be lessened. He knew that both sides were building up their nuclear arsenals with weapons that had the ability to kill millions and that an all-out war had to be avoided. So he decided to meet with the leader of the Soviet Union, Nikita S. Khrushchev, in June 1961.

The two men did not get along well, and the meeting went horribly. Khrushchev figured Kennedy would be scared and intimidated, so he chose not to be particularly flexible on any of the issues being discussed. Kennedy tried to be reasonable, tried to show that he was willing to meet Khrushchev halfway on many points, but the Soviet dictator wouldn't budge. Khrushchev insisted, for example, that communism would ultimately win out over American democracy because history was on the Soviet Union's side. But Kennedy wanted to avoid arguments over ideas and get back to the nuclear situation. With that in mind, he suggested that the two nations sign an agreement to stop testing nuclear weapons. Khrushchev, however, wanted both sides to first destroy their existing nuclear arsenals. Kennedy wasn't willing to trust Khrushchev on this point, and Khrushchev wasn't willing to trust Kennedy on the promise to stop testing.

The two leaders also disagreed on other important issues, and the meeting ended with no solutions. Indeed, Khrushchev had refused to agree to the reunification of Germany, divided since the end of World War II. In 1961 East Germany had a communist government like that of its former Soviet administrators, and West Germany, which had been administered by the United States, Britain, and France, had a democracy. The Soviets were unwilling to relinquish control of their puppet state in the east, and Kennedy suspected Khrushchev of having his eye on the more prosperous democracy in the west.

Under the circumstances, a depressed President Kennedy returned to the United States fearful that the relationship with the Soviet Union would only get worse. He was correct.

THE CUBAN MISSILE CRISIS

Just over two months after Kennedy's meeting with Khrushchev, East German authorities built a wall to separate East and West Germany. Cutting through the traditional capital city of Berlin, the barrier became known as the Berlin Wall. It was an unmistakable symbol of the cold war, and the tension between America and the Soviet Union would grow to terrifying heights in October 1962.

Fidel Castro, fearful of an invasion by the American military to compensate for the Bay of Pigs fiasco, allowed Khrushchev to move to Cuban soil Soviet-made missiles that could be armed with nuclear explosives. Cuba was a valuable location for Khrushchev because from there he could have launched a missile attack on New York, Washington, Chicago, Dallas, or Los Angeles.

On October 14 American spy planes flying over the Caribbean spotted some of the Soviet missiles, and Kennedy knew that their presence so close to American shores would have a powerful impact on ordinary citizens. "Offensive missiles in Cuba have a very different psychological and political effect in this hemisphere

German troops stand guard at the Berlin Wall in 1961.

than missiles in the USSR pointed to us," he said in a meeting with his advisers on October 22, 1962. He knew he had to do something, but which course of action would be best? If he attacked Cuba and destroyed the missiles, the Soviet Union would probably fight back, starting World War III. If Kennedy did nothing, however, the Soviets would have tremendous power over America because of the threat posed by the missiles. The president there-

THE CUBAN EMBARGO

One of the factors that drove Fidel Castro to develop a stronger relationship with the communist Soviet Union was the embargo America had placed on Cuba. An embargo is a rule declared by a government that disallows any commercial interactions between the nation setting the embargo and another nation. Kennedy had already imposed a partial embargo when Castro began taking over American-owned businesses in Cuba. After Castro responded by commandeering even more businesses, Kennedy had imposed a full trade embargo on February 7, 1962. This essentially put a stop to all trade between the United States and Cuba, which hurt Cuba's economy tremendously—America had been a huge buyer of many of Cuba's exports, including sugar, nickel, and tobacco. The embargo also outlawed American vacation travel to Cuba, delivering a massive blow to Cuba's tourist industry. Kennedy's Cuban embargo remains in effect to this day.

fore had to find a middle course that would resolve the crisis without setting off a nuclear war.

After talking with his most trusted advisers, Kennedy decided to first create a naval blockade—a series of navy ships to surround the island of Cuba and make sure Soviet ships couldn't deliver any more missiles. Then Kennedy threatened Khrushchev by saying he would, in fact, attack Cuba to destroy the missiles unless Khrushchev had them removed.

Kennedy went on television and informed the American public of the situation on October 22—and the fear of nuclear war swept across the world for the next few days. Kennedy had made his move; now it was time for Khrushchev to respond. Four days later, Khrushchev implied that he would remove the missiles—but only under two conditions. First, Kennedy had to promise not to take any military action against Cuba afterward. Second, Kennedy was to order the removal of a group of American missiles from Turkey. Part of Turkey borders the former Soviet Union. The missiles, therefore, were capable of striking several important Russian cities.

Kennedy eventually agreed to both conditions, and the threatening missiles were removed. The world breathed a sigh of relief as a war that would've killed millions was avoided. In addition, Kennedy had passed an important test, proving himself much tougher than the Soviet leader had expected. The president's handling of the matter greatly increased Kennedy's (and America's) credibility in foreign affairs.

The Cold War Thaws . . . A Little

After the Cuban missile crisis, the relationship between America and the Soviet Union began to improve somewhat. Kennedy decided to use his new credibility in foreign affairs as a way of getting Khrushchev to sign a nuclear test ban treaty—an agreement through which both nations would find safer ways to test their latest nuclear weapons, and a first step toward slowing the arms race.

In the past, nuclear weapons were tested either on the ground or over water. However, such tests often created dangerous environmental conditions. In March 1954, for example, a U.S. test of a nuclear device caused radioactive material to fall on a

Japanese fishing boat. As a result, most of the crew either became seriously ill or died. The safest way to test newly developed nuclear weapons, each side decided, was in underground facilities. This approach takes more time and is more expensive, but it doesn't pose as much of a threat to the earth.

On August 5, 1963, after working out all the details, the Soviets signed the first nuclear test ban treaty with America (plus the United Kingdom). It was considered a partial treaty, as it did not give Kennedy and the other signers everything they had hoped for. But it was a start, and it inspired similar agreements between the world's superpowers in the years ahead. Perhaps most importantly, it created a new spirit of cooperation between America and the Soviet Union, which in turn calmed global fears of nuclear war. Kennedy considered the treaty to be one of his greatest achievements.

Vietnam

By the time Kennedy became president, South Vietnamese leader Ngo Dinh Diem was asking America for more money, military equipment, and advisers. To maintain Eisenhower's policy of containing communism, Kennedy approved these requests, but he didn't want American forces to become directly involved in the fighting. The increased aid to Diem seemed to make little difference, however. Worse still, Diem was developing a reputation as a merciless dictator. Far from acting as a champion of democracy, Diem and his aides gave special favors to wealthy citizens, took part in illegal smuggling operations, and tortured and killed political enemies. Meanwhile, the average South Vietnamese person still lived a miserable life—and many wondered if they would be better off under Ho Chi Minh.

Diem's cruelty made it hard for Kennedy to continue supporting him. Kennedy pleaded with Diem to his political practices,
pointing out that it was hard for the U.S. president to continue to
support an openly antidemocratic regime. Diem ignored these
requests, however. Moreover, Diem's armies were losing the fight
against the North. Reports began arriving at the White House that
Diem was doing a poor job of commanding his generals, that there
was incompetence at every level of Diem's military, and that his soldiers were becoming disillusioned and losing their commitment to
support the government of South Vietnam.

In the summer of 1963 Kennedy and his staff began discussing the possibility of replacing Diem. Then, on November 2,
1963 the situation was resolved when several South Vietnamese
generals led a coup to remove Diem from power. The former
president was executed, along with his brother, Ngo Dinh Nhu, a
particularly cruel and ruthless individual who had been Diem's
closest adviser.

Chaos followed in the wake of Diem's removal, and Ho Chi
Minh ordered his military to increase attacks on South Vietnam to
take advantage of the situation. Nevertheless, Kennedy saw the
coup as a step in the right direction. With a better leader, he
believed, South Vietnam could eventually overtake the North
and Ho Chi Minh. And, he hoped, this would be possible without
further American involvement—he had a plan to remove all
American personnel from South Vietnam by 1965. He said at the
time, "The first thing I'm going to do when I'm re-elected [to a
second term as president], I'm going to get the Americans out of
Vietnam." Sadly, he wouldn't live to see this plan carried out.

NOVEMBER 22, 1963 *Seven*

*I*n June 1963 President Kennedy decided to visit Dallas the follow-ing November. The 1964 election would be less than a year away, and Kennedy wanted to improve his image in Texas because he and his vice president, Lyndon Johnson, had barely won the state in the 1960 election (and, in fact, had lost the popular vote in Dallas itself). Kennedy also hoped his appearance would raise money not only for his own campaign but for other Texas Democrats.

The trip was planned for November 22, with Kennedy and his wife landing at Love Field, being driven through the city of Dallas, then arriving at the Dallas Trade Mart, where he would give a luncheon speech to over 2,500 people.

Kennedy's plane landed at Love Field at 11:40 AM. By 11:55 the president and his wife were in their limousine, and the motor-cade pulled away toward downtown Dallas. There were three rows of seats in the limo. Two Secret Service agents (one driving) were in the front, Texas governor John Connally and his wife, Nellie, were in the middle, and Kennedy and the First Lady were in the back. Since it was a beautiful day, the top on the vehicle had been removed.

Thousands of people lined the Dallas streets. There were men and women alike, as well as children propped up on their parents' shoulders. Everyone was cheering and waving, and the Kennedys happily waved back. The president had been warned about possible security issues before the trip—there had been death threats, for example—but he decided to come anyway. Based on the warm reception he was receiving, he figured he had made the right choice.

President John F. Kennedy and the First Lady arrive at Love Field in Dallas.

The motorcade rolled down Main Street, surrounded by tall buildings on either side, then reached an open area called Dealey Plaza. The vehicle turned right onto Houston Street and moved toward the seven-story Texas School Book Depository, an older building that served as a warehouse for textbooks and other school supplies. Just as the motorcade reached the Depository, it turned left and headed away from it in a diagonal path along Elm Street. The time was about 12:30 PM.

When the limousine was about a third of the way down Elm Street, Nellie Connally turned to Kennedy and said, "Mr. President, they can't make you believe now that there are not some in Dallas who love you and appreciate you, can they?" Kennedy smiled and replied, "No, they sure can't." These were the last words he ever spoke.

A split second later, a sharp sound cut through the air. Most people ignored it, assuming it was either a firecracker or a muffler backfiring. Then two more shots were fired—and the president reacted. First, he clenched his hands into tight fists and brought them up to his throat. At the same time, Governor Connally pitched forward with pain on his face, and his wife pulled him down for protection. Then a shot struck President Kennedy on the right side of the head. People began pointing to one of the high windows in the School Book Depository, some saying they had seen a rifle barrel sticking out of it.

Realizing what had happened, the driver of the limousine sped off to nearby Parkland Memorial Hospital. In spite of all efforts to save Kennedy, however, too much damage had been done—he was pronounced dead at 1:00 PM. Less than two hours later, Lyndon Johnson was sworn in as the thirty-sixth president.

Moments after this photograph was taken, President Kennedy was assassinated as his car passed through Dealey Plaza in Dallas, Texas, on November 22, 1963.

LEE HARVEY OSWALD

Not long after the shooting, Dallas police get word that Lee Harvey Oswald, one of the people who worked in the School Book Depository, was missing. Oswald was a former U.S. Marine with an excellent record of marksmanship. In October 1959 he had moved to the Soviet Union, saying he would rather be a communist than an American. By June 1962, however, he had returned to the United States, where he moved to Texas and began working in a variety of jobs—mostly because he couldn't hold onto one for long. He also lived briefly in New Orleans and in Mexico City, returning to Dallas in October 1963.

Oswald was captured by Dallas police in a local movie theater less than two hours after President Kennedy's assassination. Interestingly, he wasn't arrested for shooting the president, but for killing a police officer named J. D. Tippit, who had spotted him on a suburban street and wanted to question him. But then, on the sixth floor of the School Book Depository, a rifle was

Accused of the assassination of President Kennedy, Lee Harvey Oswald is escorted through the Dallas police department.

found—the one that had shot the president. The police soon discovered that the weapon belonged to Oswald, who was then charged with killing both Tippit and President Kennedy. Oswald denied the accusations, but the evidence was overwhelming.

Then the case took another unbelievable turn. While Oswald was being escorted from the Dallas police station to the vehicle that was to take him to the county jail, a man named Jack Ruby—a nightclub owner in the Dallas area—stepped out of the surrounding crowd and shot Oswald in the abdomen. Incredibly, all this was being broadcast live on national TV, and Americans were left speechless for the second

CONSPIRACY?

Through the years, thousands of people have entertained the theory that Oswald did not act alone when he killed President Kennedy but was part of a larger conspiracy. Some believe Fidel Castro may have been involved, carrying out revenge for Kennedy's attempt to overthrow his regime in the Bay of Pigs. Others think the assassination might have been ordered by Khrushchev, embarrassed by his loss of credibility during the Cuban missile crisis. There is even a belief that certain high-ranking members of the American military were behind the killing to stop Kennedy from putting an end to America's involvement in Vietnam. However, no evidence has come to light to prove any of these conspiracy theories, and the official judgment remains that Lee Harvey Oswald was the president's sole assassin.

time in as many days. Oswald quickly lost consciousness and died less than two hours later.

THE LEGACY OF JOHN FITZGERALD KENNEDY

On Monday, November 25, millions watched on television as Kennedy's funeral procession moved through the streets of Washington, D.C. His wife, dressed in black, held the hands of Caroline and John Jr. and bravely kept her emotions in check. Shortly after 3:30, the president's coffin was lowered into the ground at Arlington National Cemetery, and a flame was lit on the grave that burns to this day.

John F. Kennedy Jr. and sister Caroline stand by their mother after the funeral service of their father at St. Matthew's Cathedral in Washington, D.C.

In spite of the tragic nature of John Kennedy's death, it is far outweighed by the positive aspects of his life. He was a man of great energy and compassion, of tremendous wit and charm. In spite of his health problems, he drove himself to amazing achievements. He was a loving father, a charming husband, a faithful son, and a loyal brother. He always put the interests of America first, as his devotion to his country was unmistakable. As a member of the House of Representatives and then the Senate, he fought for the rights of working people in his home state of Massachusetts. As president, he valiantly battled the threat of communism around the world and may have singlehandedly averted a nuclear war. He proved that a young man could master a supremely difficult job, and he carried an immeasurable faith in humanity. No task was too big, no challenge too great, and no obstacle too high.

As he said in a speech at Washington's American University a few months before his death, "Our problems are manmade, therefore they may be solved by man. And man can be as big as he wants. No problem of human destiny is beyond human beings."

For many, John F. Kennedy is viewed as one of the nation's most compelling leaders during a time of tremendous change in U.S. history.

1917
John Fitzgerald Kennedy is born on May 29 in Brookline, Massachusetts

1936
Begins taking classes at Harvard University

1942
Assigned to command a PT boat in World War II

1946
Elected to the U.S. House of Representatives

1910

1952
Elected to the U.S. Senate

1953
Marries Jacqueline Bouvier
on September 12

1960
Elected president of the
United States

1963
Assassinated on November
22 in Dallas, Texas

1970

NOTES

CHAPTER 1

p. 8, ". . . was similar to Pat in both temperament and ethics . . ." Ted Schwarz, *Joseph P. Kennedy: The Mogul, the Mob, the Statesman, and the Making of an American Myth*. Hoboken, NJ: John Wiley & Sons, 2003, p. 40.

p. 10, ". . . it's not only that I want to look that way . . ." quoted in Robert Dallek, *An Unfinished Life: John F. Kennedy, 1917–1963*. Boston: Little, Brown, 2003, p. 37.

p. 11, ". . . the more I talk with him, the more confidence I have in him . . ." quoted in Dallek, *An Unfinished Life*, p. 40.

p. 13, "Joe Kennedy was a greedy man . . ." Schwarz, *Joseph P. Kennedy*, p. 163.

CHAPTER 2

p. 18, ". . . the Peace Treaty was imposed . . ." Adolf Hitler and James Vincent Murphy (translator), *Mein Kampf*. Amsterdam, The Netherlands: Fredonia Classics, 2003, p. 513.

p. 22, ". . . worked hard at it because I liked PTs . . ." quoted in Ralph G. Martin, *A Hero for Our Time: An Intimate Story of the Kennedy Years*. New York: Macmillan, 1983, p. 43.

p. 24, ". . . those men would do anything . . ." quoted in Martin, *A Hero for Our Time*, p. 43.

p. 27, ". . . one of the most severe shocks . . ." Arthur Krock, *Memoirs: Intimate Recollections of Twelve American Presidents, from Theodore Roosevelt to Richard Nixon*. London: Cassell, 1970, p. 324.

CHAPTER 3

p. 30, "He was always shy, . . ." quoted in Dallek, *An Unfinished Life*, p. 119.

p. 33, "I've given up arguing with him, . . ." quoted in Thomas C. Reeves, *A Question of Character: The Life of John F. Kennedy*. New York: Free Press, 1991, p. 92.

p. 37, ". . . wasn't equipped for the job. I didn't plan to get into it . . ." quoted in Dallek, *An Unfinished Life*, p. 137.

p. 40, "They don't have to like me, . . ." quoted in Martin, *A Hero for Our Time*, p. 58.

CHAPTER 4

p. 46, "It's the most corrupting job" quoted in Dallek, *An Unfinished Life*, p. 177.

p. 49, ". . . rather die than spend the rest of my life . . ." quoted in Michael O'Brien, *John F. Kennedy: A Biography*. New York: Thomas Dunne Books, 2005, p. 279.

p. 50, ". . . believed that telling the stories . . ." quoted in John F. Kennedy (primary author) and Caroline Kennedy (Introduction author), *Profiles in Courage*. New York: HarperCollins, 2004, p. xii.

p. 61, ". . . don't see how the Flint High School football team . . ." quoted in Bill Adler (editor and compiler), *The Kennedy Wit*. New York: Citadel Press, 1964, p. 9.

CHAPTER 5

p. 65, ". . . ask not what your country can do for you . . ." quoted in Thurston Clarke (editor and compiler), *Ask Not: The Inauguration of John F. Kennedy and the Speech That Changed America*. New York: Macmillan, 2004, p. xvi.

p. 66, ". . . this nation should commit itself to achieving the goal . . ." Speech delivered to Congress, May 25, 1961. "Special Message to the Congress on Urgent National Needs, Page 4," www.jfklibrary.org/Historical+Resources/Archives/Reference +Desk/Speeches/JFK/Urgent+National+Needs+Page+4.htm (accessed October 15, 2008).

p. 72, ". . . took some modest steps early in the administration . . ." Reeves, *A Question of Character*, p. 337.

p. 73, ". . . once asked what her father was doing . . ." O'Brien, *John F. Kennedy*, p. 745.

CHAPTER 6

p. 77, " . . . one of the most sensitive and difficult assignments . . ." quoted in Martin, *A Hero for Our Time*, pp. 369–370.

p. 79, ". . . to complete the revolution of the Americas . . ." quoted in Reeves, *A Question of Character*, 1991, p. 359.

p. 81, ". . . loss of life during the Bay of Pigs invasion . . ." Clarke, *Ask Not*, p. 189.

p. 84, ". . . missiles in Cuba have a very different psychological and political effect . . ." quoted in Ernest R. May and Philip Zelikow, *The Kennedy Tapes: Inside the White House During the Cuban Missile Crisis*. New York: W. W. Norton, 2002, p. 159.

p. 88, ". . . first thing I'm going to do . . ." quoted in Martin, *A Hero for Our Time*, p. 500.

CHAPTER 7

p. 91, ". . . they can't make you believe now . . ." quoted in Vincent Bugliosi, *Reclaiming History: The Assassination of President John F. Kennedy*. New York: W. W. Norton, 2007, p. 37.

p. 96, "Our problems are manmade, . . ." From the 'Commencement Address at American University,' given on June 10, 1963, www.jfklibrary.org/Historical+Resources/ Archives/Reference+Desk/Speeches/JFK/003POF03AmericanUniversity06101963. htm (accessed October 15, 2008).

GLOSSARY

Camelot the royal court of the legendary King Arthur; used to describe the "feel" of the White House during the Kennedy administration

capitalism the economic system in which most of the businesses are owned by private citizens rather than by the government

cold war the period of tension between the United States and the Soviet Union following World War II

communism the social system in which people put their individual rights and freedoms second to the benefits of their community, which are agreed to be for the greater good

Democratic Party the more liberal of the two major political parties in the United States

domestic in politics, having to do with one's home country

Great Depression the period of worldwide economic stagnation that began with the October 1929 stock market crash in America

House of Representatives one of the two chambers of the U.S. Congress. There are currently 435 members.

last rites Roman Catholic practice of praying for and anointing a person who has died or is believed to be close to death

policy a specific course of action or attitude toward a subject or issue

Republican Party the more conservative of the two major political parties in the United States

Senate the upper chamber of the U.S. Congress. There are currently one hundred members, two from each state.

FURTHER INFORMATION

BOOKS

Aronson, Billy. *Richard M. Nixon*. New York: Marshall Cavendish Benchmark, 2008.

Brown Agins, Donna. *Jacqueline Kennedy Onassis: Legendary First Lady*. Berkeley Heights, NJ: Enslow, 2004.

Byrne, Paul J. *The Cuban Missile Crisis*. Mankato, MN: Compass Point Books, 2006.

Hodge, Marie. *John F. Kennedy: Voice of Hope*. New York: Sterling, 2007.

Marcovitz, Hal. *The Vietnam War*. Farmington Hills, MI: Lucent Books, 2007.

DVD

Biography: John F. Kennedy, A Personal Story. A&E Home Video, 2005.

WEB SITES

John F. Kennedy Presidential Library and Museum

www.jfklibrary.org/

Official site of the John F. Kennedy Library and Presidential Museum. Loads of excellent content, beautifully presented. Suitable for all ages.

Peace Corps

www.peacecorps.gov/

Home page of the Peace Corps. Comprehensive information about the organization that President Kennedy launched in 1961.

The Cold War Museum

www.coldwar.org/

A kid-friendly site that covers all aspects of the cold war period between the United States and the Soviet Union. Includes a trivia game, information about well-known spies of the era, personal stories, and a "traveling museum."

The White House: John Kennedy

www.whitehouse.gov/history/presidents/jk35.html

Official White House page for John F. Kennedy. Gives basic information.

BIBLIOGRAPHY

Adler, Bill (editor and compiler), *The Kennedy Wit*. New York: Citadel Press, 1964.

Bugliosi, Vincent. *Reclaiming History: The Assassination of President John F. Kennedy*. New York: W. W. Norton, 2007.

Clarke, Thurston (editor and compiler), *Ask Not: The Inauguration of John F. Kennedy and the Speech That Changed America*. New York: Macmillan, 2004.

Dallek, Robert. *An Unfinished Life: John F. Kennedy, 1917–1963*. Boston: Little, Brown, 2003.

Harrison, Barbara, and Daniel Terris. *A Twilight Struggle: The Life of John Fitzgerald Kennedy*. New York: Lothrop, Lee & Shepard, 1992.

Hitler, Adolf, and James Vincent Murphy (translator), *Mein Kampf*. Amsterdam, The Netherlands: Fredonia Classics, 2003.

Kennedy, John F. (primary author), and Caroline Kennedy (Introduction author), *Profiles in Courage*. New York: HarperCollins, 2004.

Krock, Arthur. *Memoirs of Intimate Recollections of American Presidents, from Theodore Roosevelt to Richard Nixon*. London: Cassell, 1970.

Martin, Ralph G. *A Hero for Our Time: An Intimate Story of the Kennedy Years*. New York: Macmillan, 1983.

May, Ernest R., and Philip Zelikow. *The Kennedy Tapes: Inside the White House During the Cuban Missile Crisis*. New York: W. W. Norton, 2002.

O'Brien, Michael. *John F. Kennedy: A Biography*. New York: Thomas Dunne Books, 2005.

Perret, Geoffrey. *Eisenhower*. New York: Random House, 1999.

Reeves, Thomas C. *A Question of Character: The Life of John F. Kennedy*. New York: The Free Press, 1991.

Schlesinger, Jr., Arthur M. *A Thousand Days: John F. Kennedy in the White House*. Boston: Houghton Mifflin, 1965.

Schwarz, Ted. *Joseph P. Kennedy: The Mogul, the Mob, the Statesman, and the Making of an American Myth*. Hoboken, NJ: John Wiley & Sons, 2003.

Sorensen, Theodore C. *Kennedy*. New York: Harper & Row, 1965.

INDEX

Pages in **boldface** are illustrations.

ABOUT THE AUTHOR

Wil Mara is the author of more than ninety books. Many are reference titles for young readers. For Marshall Cavendish Benchmark he wrote *John Adams* and *Gerald Ford* in the Presidents and Their Times series. More information about his work, including a complete bibliography, can be found at www.wilmara.com.